BRITAIN IN OLD PHOTOGRAPHS

AROUND
CARLISLE

ELIZABETH NELSON

SUTTON PUBLISHING LIMITED

Sutton Publishing Limited
Phoenix Mill · Thrupp · Stroud
Gloucestershire · GL5 2BU

First published 1997

Cover photographs: *front*; Mr W. Wilson and
his staff at his shoeing forge in West Walls,
Carlisle: *back*; D. Asti and his ice-cream van,
c. 1920.

British Library Cataloguing in Publication Data
A catalogue record for this book is available from the
British Library.

ISBN 0-7509-1361-4

Typeset in 10/12 Perpetua.
Typesetting and origination by
Sutton Publishing Limited.
Printed in Great Britain by
Ebenezer Baylis, Worcester.

CONTENTS

It was all very well to be put in the pillory for fun at a Gala, as sometimes was the case, but not much fun to be there for all passersby to mock and jeer at, with no prospect of release until the punishment was complete. Perhaps this was an effective treatment! This pillory is kept in the city, though without the present occupants.

INTRODUCTION

Standing in its strategic position in the northern corner of England, close to the Scottish border, Carlisle was fought over by successive kings of England and Scotland long before King Henry II gave the city its first charter in 1158. Not that this brought peace; border conflict continued for many centuries with five bays of the cathedral damaged during the Civil War in 1646.

The history of the city since the days of the Roman occupation has been well documented, and once photography became a medium to be reckoned with a large pictorial record has been established. I was reluctant to add yet another publication to the fascinating books that have already been published, but with photographs of my own and others not previously seen I felt I could show something slightly different regarding the inhabitants and the work that has been done in the city throughout the twentieth century.

Some buildings and streets have disappeared during the modernization of the town but the cathedral, castle and Carlisle Cross in the market square remain as they have done for hundreds of years. Churches have come and gone as populations spread further out from the centre and have subsequently sprung up in the suburbs. Through the ages kings and queens have visited Carlisle, perhaps not always as welcome as members of the Royal family are today. Their coronations and jubilees have been reason for great celebration and it was very exciting for the city to have the Royal Maundy service there in 1978.

As a market town Carlisle has enjoyed prosperity of late and I have tried to show some of the shops and businesses that made up the life of the city and a glimpse of a few of the many factories that ensured employment for the majority of people living in the area. The care for those less fortunate than ourselves has been an attribute here as in every place.

Carlisle has a long musical tradition with the cathedral organ and choir, and choral societies and well-known soloists. Brass bands were always popular while St Stephen's Silver Band had the honour of winning the British Bank Federation trophy twice. The secondary modern schools now fulfil the needs of most children but once there were a number of private schools, some of which I have tried to show. The sporting activities of the district are also described. Here, as everywhere, football is a great sport and the ups and downs of Carlisle United are followed with tremendous enthusiasm.

Carlisle is proud of its long and important railway position which has been the source of much employment. Although modern trains do not have the nostalgia of travel a century ago, they have brought speed and cleanliness with the change. It is probably in travel that this century has witnessed more development than in any other. The crowds who flocked to see the early aircraft would now not raise their heads if jumbo jets or tornados roared above them. Today's cars may be dependable and certainly far faster but do motorists miss the thrill of those early days when the car had to be cranked to start, some adjustment done under the bonnet and punctures were commonplace? Arrival was always an achievement!

It was always the small events that were the most memorable. In those years during the Second World War, in spite of the shortages, the blackout and the anxiety – or perhaps because of them – there was a tremendous spirit of comradeship in that everyone was working towards a common aim. We felt safe wherever we walked, even in the darkest days.

The years of animosity and border warfare are, we hope, gone forever and all who come to our city come in friendship; we welcome them as we hope they would welcome us. Carlisle has expanded in all directions and modern technology has changed the work pattern but it still stands at the gateway to Scotland.

I have tried to depict something of the spirit of the people in and around Carlisle over the last century. We cannot stand still and change has to come, but I am certain that the same spirit that has stood these people in good stead through two world wars and has not been deterred by the changes of the last hundred years will see the future, whatever it may hold, as a challenge, and meet it with resilience.

THE BORDER CITY

Carlisle Cross standing in the market square in the time of Bonnie Prince Charlie. It still stands today, surmounted by the carved lion holding a stone copy of the Dormant Book across its paws. This elaborately bound book belongs to the Corporation and contains, along with matters of a later date, the by-laws of the city from the government of 1561. There are sundials on each side of the block surmounting the plinth on top of which the lion sits. Since the granting of the first charter to the city in 1158 the Great Fair has been proclaimed from the cross in August, even during the years when the fair itself stopped. In 1975 it was revived and for a week the market square is packed with stalls of all descriptions and entertainments of all kinds.

The Guildhall in the 1730s, facing the market square with Fisher Street leading down the right-hand side. Built in the fifteenth century, the Guildhall is one of the oldest buildings in the city and is sometimes called Redness Hall after Richard de Redness, who once lived there. The banners of the different guilds, whose meeting place it was, used to be displayed from the windows on Ascension Day.

The Guildhall, seen here in about 1910, was later occupied by the baby linen and ladies' underclothing department of J. Huthart & Co. Ltd, General Drapers. Other departments were on the opposite side of Fisher Street, on the right of this picture. An old established firm, they had a good reputation gained from nigh on a century of supplying sound, reliable goods.

A coach and horses makes its way through the Scotch Gate of the City, at the northern end of Scotch Street. The rooms above this gate were at one time used as a prison, latterly as a debtor's prison until 1790. It was demolished in 1815.

Work in full progress on the new Carlisle market which was begun in 1887 to the design of Cawston and Graham. It was completed in 1889. The large roof was made by Cowans Sheldon & Co., Carlisle, and their trade plate is still visible.

An aerial view of Carlisle taken 300 feet up from the top of Dixon's chimney. The brewery is to the front, on the left, with the River Caldew and Caldew Bridge in the foreground. The River Eden winds across the upper part of the picture with Eden Bridge on the right and Stanwix visible in the centre at the back. The castle dominates the picture and the West Walls of the city can be seen rising up in front of the houses on the right.

The hustle and bustle of the open market as crowds throng the stalls in the market square in front of the Town Hall, c. 1890. Scotch Street leads down on the right of the Town Hall.

Carlisle from Dixon's chimney.
300 feet high.

A continuation of the picture on the previous page, looking over the city from the top of Dixon's chimney. In the foreground the large number of railway lines show the important part they played in the life of the city. Behind the lines the West Walls rise to the front of the houses. To the centre right the cathedral is dominant, giving an idea of the immense area it would have covered if the five bays, destroyed by the Scots in 1646, had still been standing. The Deanery is built on to West Walls and the fratry, or refectory in its Priory days, lies between it and the cathedral; St Mary's Church is to the right. In the top left can be seen the bridge going north over the River Eden, while the river wends its way upstream along the back of the picture.

The billboard men used to be a familiar sight: Mayco Margarine was 1s per pound, The Very Best Tea 1s 4d per lb, with a reliable blend at 1s 2d. These are a reminder of prices in about 1910. The Town Hall clock is just visible at the top left-hand side. One wonders how the long dresses of the ladies, as they head down Scotch Street, would fare as they came into contact with the deposits of the horses prevalent in those days.

St Cuthbert's Lane looking towards the market square which is visible in the distance. On the left is the Fish and Dolphin public house, one of the many hostelries closed down when the state management took control of liquor licensing in 1916.

The entrance hall to the public library in Castle Street. This was part of the extensions to Tullie House completed in 1893. The stairs on the left led to rooms used for art exhibitions and meetings, the door ahead into the library itself. All the rooms were incorporated into a much enlarged Tullie House Museum after the library moved into a new building in the city centre Lanes development in 1986.

The interior of the Fish and Dolphin public house in about 1905, the windows overlooking St Cuthbert's Lane.

One of the few parts of the city walls to survive, this section of West Walls has changed little from when this picture was taken in the early days of the century. The back of the Deanery, the large house in the centre, is built up to the road and just off the picture there are steps down to a walk below, which now lead to the town Dyke Orchard car park. Cars travelling in both directions now do so with difficulty in the limited passing places.

The market-place looks positively empty without the market in progress. The open-topped tram makes its way along the street and, although pony and trap was still a common form of transport, motorized vehicles were appearing when this picture was taken in about 1920. The statue of James Steel, twice mayor of Carlisle and editor of the *Carlisle Journal*, erected in 1859, is in the foreground.

Looking into the city from the Victoria viaduct which was opened on 20 September 1877, by HRH the Princess Louise. It carried traffic over the railway and the River Caldew to connect with Denton Holme. The large building in the centre is the premises of Little & Ballantyne, the well-known nurserymen and seed merchants. The Central Hotel can be seen on the right.

The visitor's first view of Carlisle on leaving the railway station is of the Court Houses standing guard on either side of English Street. Originally built in 1542 the two houses were joined by fortified buildings to guard the southern approach to the city. They were converted into court houses in about 1810, and approximately a hundred years later horse-drawn cabs wait in their shadow for fares emerging from the station. The modern taxi still stands in much the same position today.

A solitary tram makes its way up Botchergate with a young cyclist pedalling hard to beat it as he turns right into The Crescent. The entrance to Redmaynes, the tailors, is on the left, with what was the Red Lion Hotel on the upper floors of that building. The Midland Bank Chambers are on the right and the canopy, extending over the pavement, belongs to the entrance to the County and Station Hotel ballroom, slightly further down Botchergate on the right.

Rickergate, at the northern end of Scotch Street and leading down to the River Eden, was a bustling thoroughfare at the turn of the century. Jardine, Carruthers & Sons on the left were well-known ironmongers and manufacturers of shoe plates and clogs.

Going on from Rickergate two pedal cyclists have crossed Eden Bridge, erected over the river in 1815, and are climbing up to Stanwix. This scene dates from the latter part of the nineteenth century, before the laying of tram lines in 1900. The cathedral behind the houses on the left-hand side rises to the skyline while Dixon's chimney points like a massive flag-pole from the centre of the castle on the right.

ALL THINGS SPIRITUAL

A girl obligingly pauses for the camera as she pushes the baby past St Cuthbert's Church along Blackfriars Street, named after the friars who were housed there. St Cuthbert's, the city church of Carlisle where the mayor and corporation attend one Sunday service after each mayoral inauguration, was originally only one of two churches serving the city, its parish boundaries extending to Blackwell, Upperby and Carleton.

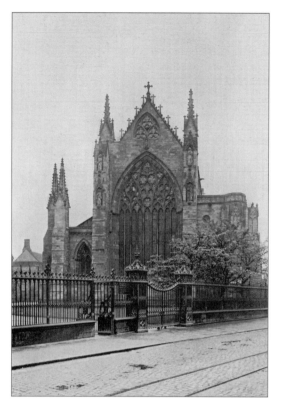

Looking towards the east end of the cathedral from Castle Street. The splendid railings, designed in 1838 by R.W. Billings, separate the grounds from the street. These were a contentious issue and were taken down in 1930. They were regarded as an eyesore by some and a distinguished feature by others.

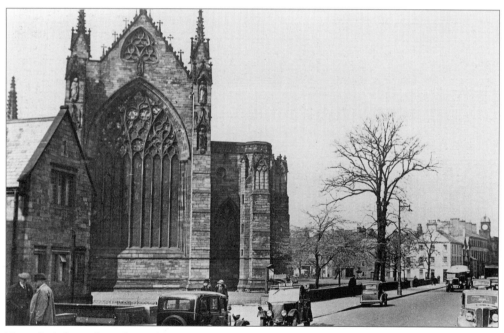

The cathedral seen from almost the same angle but without the railings in the mid-1930s. On the extreme left is the house of the head verger, and in the distance on the right Tullie House clock stands out.

The choir of Carlisle Cathedral looking towards the magnificent east window. This measures 51 ft by 26 ft and contains both medieval and Victorian glass. It is considered to be one of the finest in the county. The Paley Memorial pulpit is on the left. On the right can be seen part of a small temporary organ installed while renovation work was undertaken on the very fine Willis organ in 1907.

A delightful picture of the Right Reverend Cyril Bulley, Lord Bishop of Carlisle, 1967–1972, and the Venerable Charles Nurse, Archdeacon of Carlisle, 1958–1970, greeting each other as they meet in the fratry, Carlisle Cathedral. The fratry, standing on the south side of the cathedral, is a separate building which was erected at the end of the fifteenth century. This was the refectory in the priory before the Dissolution.

The parish of St Mary, which served the northern part of the city, had the nave of the cathedral as its place of worship, a wall at one time dividing the nave from the choir and transepts. In 1870 a parish church of St Mary's was built at the east end of the cathedral grounds. St Mary's was a fine church but with the building of other churches in the suburbs to which the population were moving, there was not the same demand for places of worship in the city centre. In the 1930s St Mary's was amalgamated with St Paul's and later demolished.

Five of the seven bays of the nave of Carlisle
Cathedral were destroyed by the Scots army in
1646 but the two that remain show how
strongly they were built in preparation for
resisting northern invaders. In the centre,
between the columns, is now the chapel of the
Border Regiment.

St Stephen's Church in James Street was built in 1865 in an area that was fast developing industrially, with
small houses also being built. A fine church with a good musical tradition, it is here decorated in all its
glory for the harvest festival of 1908.

The laying of the foundation stone of St Aidan's Church in Warwick Road on 20 September 1899, by the Duchess of Devonshire. On her left is the Lord Bishop of Carlisle, who dedicated the stone, and to her right can be seen the mayor of Carlisle and other dignitaries. The completed building was consecrated in 1901, the same year in which the foundation stone was laid for the connecting church hall on the northern side of the church. This stone was laid by Mrs Catherine Blanchard, by whose munificence the hall was erected.

A little girl awaits the tram heading for the city, as the two trams meet at their passing place opposite St Aidan's Church. This picture was probably taken in the 1920s.

Rather higher up Warwick Road towards the city the trams passed the Catholic church of Our Lady and St Joseph which was consecrated in 1893. This is a fine church with the presbytery adjoining on the south side and a large church hall in Warwick Square, the road on the bottom right.

A Roman Catholic mass being celebrated outdoors. It is obviously a very important occasion for the children sitting in the front, being their First Communion service.

The chapel of the Cumberland Infirmary, Carlisle, c. 1930. It is still as meaningful a place today as it was then for patients who are mobile enough to attend services there. The spiritual needs of those unable to go to the chapel are well catered for by the chaplains of all denominations.

The old-established Mission of Work for the Deaf and Dumb still carries on today at their headquarters in Compton Street, Carlisle. The chapel is a central part of the life of the Mission as is obvious from the preparation for the harvest thanksgiving, shown here on 10 October 1931.

The band and members of the congregation line up outside the Salvation Army barracks, beside the entrance to Carlisle Castle, not many years after it was built in 1895. The site had cost £1,000 and the building a further £4,000. In preparation for the inner ring road, which was built in 1977, the barracks and all property leading to Caldew Bridge had to be pulled down, almost immediately after the Salvation Army had moved into new premises in Abbey Street.

A packed congregation listen intently to Pastor Robert Tweed, a man who made his mark on the Elim Church in West Walls, Carlisle, during his time as minister there from 1929 to 1931. The Pentecostal churches were in the ascendancy and Pastor Tweed's preaching drew many to come and hear him.

The horse-drawn Church Army van, proclaiming 'GOD IS LOVE', standing in a farmyard at Upperby in 1908. The van was a temporary home for the two captains, and the small pet one of them is holding, as they went round the parish conducting meetings. The bicycle propped up against the van shows another of their forms of transport. In those days Upperby was regarded as a village and the parish was mostly rural. Today the work of the Church Army is carried on with a double-decker bus so the whole of the diocese can be easily reached.

As Carlisle expanded the need for a burial ground away from the city centre became very apparent. Land was purchased by Dalston Road, grounds were laid out and chapels built. The first burial took place in 1855, the procession coming through this arch of the entrance building.

ROYAL OCCASIONS

Her Royal Highness the Princess Louise, daughter of Queen Victoria, visited Carlisle on 24 September 1908. Here she is driving up Castle Street, accompanied by the Earl of Lonsdale, on her return from the infirmary, the cathedral visible in the centre background. Her visit aroused great excitement, judging by the large crowds lining the street.

The horse-drawn tram, offering space to let for advertisements, heads under the triumphal arch. This was specially erected between the Court Houses for the celebrations of Queen Victoria's Diamond Jubilee. Beneath her photo is written 'God Bless Our Queen'.

On the opposite side of the arch, looking south towards Court Square, the motto of the city, 'Be Just and Fear Not', is written under the coat of arms and below that, 'A Long and Glorious Reign'.

'Sixty Years a Glorious Reign', between 1837 and 1897, beneath a photograph of Queen Victoria, is proudly displayed on the decorated arch at the Irish gate city entrance from Caldewgate, looking along Annetwell Street.

An equally decorated arch was erected at the north end of Scotch Street. The market entrance, with B. Scott & Sons, Perth, is on the left and Campbell & Co., Dye Works, are on the right with 'Cocoa Rooms' on the overhanging lamp.

Crowds throng the market square on a cold and wet day on 26 January 1901, to hear the proclamation of
King Edward VII from the Town Hall.

The Freedom of the City was presented to Prince Christian on 7 July 1902. After the ceremony in the
Town Hall the Prince left with the civic party for Bitts Park to attend the Royal Show, which was being
held in Carlisle that year.

On 18 May 1917, King George V and Queen Mary paid an official visit to Carlisle, the first by a reigning monarch for 300 years. The royal cars await their return as they are received by the civic leaders in the Town Hall. Here they also met nurses and wounded soldiers.

The final visit of the day by King George and Queen Mary was to the Gretna Tavern in Lowther Street. This was the first new public house and coffee room set up by the State Management Scheme when they took over the control of all licensed premises in 1916.

On their arrival in the city, the first stop for the King and Queen had been at Edenside, where they reviewed the 1st Cumberland Volunteers and the King took the salute.

The Silver Jubilee of King George V and Queen Mary on 6 May 1935 was a great cause for celebration throughout the country. All ages join in the party spirit in this group at Belle Vue, Carlisle.

Only two years after the Silver Jubilee celebrations, festivities were in full swing for the coronation of King George VI and Queen Elizabeth. Carlisle Town Hall was proudly decorated for the occasion. The railings in the foreground surrounded the steps leading down to the underground conveniences for men and women. This island in the centre of the market square was sometimes jocularly referred to as 'Bog Island'.

Bank Street looking east, arrayed with decorations for the coronation. The parked cars are a reminder of the days when it was possible to stop outside any shop or office.

The arch between the Court Houses is perhaps not quite so spectacular in 1937 as it was in 1897 for Queen Victoria's Jubilee, but now there would be more traffic, including double-decker buses.

The coronation decorations at the corner of the Viaduct and English Street included a large crown suspended over the centre of the crossing. The picture is taken facing down the length of Devonshire Street.

A large, gaily coloured ball was the centrepiece of the decorations at the southern end of Lowther Street.
The entrance to Warwick Road is on the extreme right of the picture.

Another crown was suspended at St Nicholas at the southern entrance to the city, looking up Botchergate.
The relatively traffic-free streets enabled cyclists to travel in safety in those days.

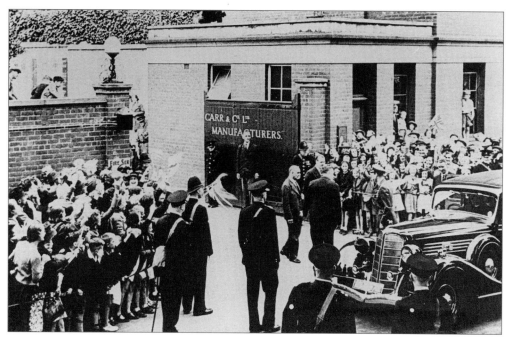

HRH the Duke of Kent arriving for a visit at the biscuit works of Carr & Co. in Caldewgate in 1941. For very many years the firm has enjoyed the Royal Warrant. Schoolchildren excitedly cheer the royal visitor although the stringencies of war limited the number of older spectators who could watch.

HRH the Princess Margaret came to Carlisle in August 1951 to attend the Pageant, which was held on Bitts Park, and also toured the Trades Exhibition in the Market Hall. Colonel Ronald Carr explains points of interest to her as he escorts her round the stand of Carr & Co., Biscuit Manufacturers. The first Pageant, depicting the history of Carlisle in nine specially written scenes, was performed in 1928 in Bitts Park, the area north of Carlisle Castle. In 1951 a similar event was held in the same place.

On 18 September 1987, Princess Margaret, president of the NSPCC, came to Carlisle to open the headquarters of the recently established Child Protection Team for Carlisle and Eden. Richard Gascoyne, Regional Organizer (hidden behind the Princess) is presenting the local officials to Her Royal Highness. From left to right they are: Bernard Stout, chairman of the North Cumbria branch, Mrs Elizabeth Nelson, vice-chairman and author, Mrs Margaret Dickenson, secretary, and Mrs P. Gordon Duff-Pennington, president of the West Cumbria branch.

On Thursday 23 March 1978, Her Majesty the Queen came to Carlisle for the distribution of the Royal Maundy. Accompanied by HRH the Duke of Edinburgh, the Queen waves to the crowds in Court Square after alighting from the royal train, before the short drive to the cathedral.

Before leaving the city the Royal visitors called at the Civic Centre. Although rain had begun to fall by this time there were plenty of large umbrellas to protect the visitors.

After the service the official party lined up outside the cathedral for the photographers. The Queen is flanked by two schoolchildren selected from local schools for the important role of Children of Royal Almonry. On the queen's right, beyond the boy, is the Dean of Carlisle, the Very Reverend John Churchill, and on her left, the Lord Bishop of Carlisle, the Right Reverend David Halsey. Behind Her Majesty stands the Lord High Almoner, the Lord Bishop of Rochester, the Right Reverend David Say. The members of the Yeomen of the Guard, who had been on duty throughout the service, are lined up on either side of the cathedral entrance.

THE CITY AT WORK

It would not be difficult to imagine the confusion today if a flock of sheep was driven along Lowther Street as this one is in the 1920s. They are probably going down to the Sands. The drover does not appear to be having any traffic problems. The Liberal Club is on the right-hand side, in the same place as it is today, and the entrance to Devonshire Street is just beyond the second parked car.

W.H. Smith & Son, booksellers and newsagents, were in this shop in English Street, between Devonshire Street and the Lowther Arcade, before moving along English Street, nearer to the market square, into new premises in 1928. Although altered over the years, these are the premises they still occupy.

Three doors further south from W.H. Smith was Dand's. Mr Dand was a harness- and trunk-maker and had a fascinating shop selling every kind of leather and sporting gear, including football boots. In the days before plastic and synthetic goods, real leather was always in demand. Mr W. Dand, a familiar figure in the shop, lived at Currock Villa.

The pharmacy at 16 Scotland Road, Stanwix, originally belonged to Ridley's, the old established firm of chemists, some of the family living at 18 Scotland Road. No. 16 would have been a private house when it was first built, the ornamental balustrade around the upstairs window still remaining, but it was converted into a shop in 1898. Mr Errington, a pharmacist with Ridley's, took it over for some years but in 1952 Mr G. Lightfoot acquired the business. Recently the shop moved to the opposite side of Scotland Road and the premises have now become Almond's Bistro.

The staff of Watson's, who were renowned for making clogs, gather outside the shop at 17 Scotch Street in 1925. They are, from left to right, Bobby Bell, Bobby Bolton, Teddy Watson (a son of the owner), Tom Watson (owner), Stanley David Monroe Watson (a son), and Billy Irving. The business was started in the 1870s by Tom Watson's father in premises further north in Scotch Street, the other side of East Tower Street. Tom's father died when Tom was only twelve years of age but his mother, Mrs Betsy Watson, carried on the business until he was able to take over. They moved to these premises in 1922, it having previously been a public house, and continued to trade here until the business closed in 1979. Clogs were a common form of footware for workers in rural areas and they did a brisk trade. In addition to clogs, Teddy also specialized in shoe repairs.

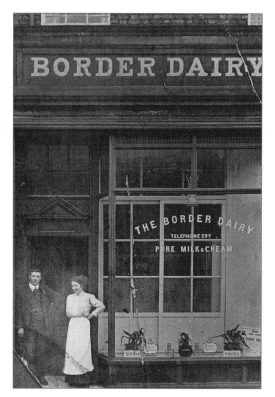

Mr and Mrs McQuillin outside their shop at 48 Lowther Street, Carlisle, *c.* 1911. They had started the Border Dairy Company in 1898, selling butter and new laid eggs as well as milk and cream. In 1935 they expanded to larger, modern premises in Shaddongate but they kept the original shop on as a retail outlet until 1960. The business as a whole was sold to the Milk Marketing Board in 1974–5.

In the days when cycling was one of the most common forms of transport, the shop to buy cycles and all things appertaining to them was very popular. One such place was J.J. Foster & Son's in Rickergate, seen here in about 1930. The site of this shop is now part of the Civic Centre.

Robinson's grocer's shop, which also served as the post office, at 125 Denton Street, Denton Holme, in 1940. The post office started up in Denton Holme on 2 April 1878, on the opposite side of the street. It moved twice more in Denton Street before being taken over by William Robinson at no. 127. In 1934 Thomas Robinson enlarged the business into the adjoining shop and it remains there still.

The staff of the Maypole Dairy Company Ltd in their shop on the corner of English Street and the Victoria viaduct, which they occupied from early this century until about 1923. They then moved to the opposite side of English Street before moving into Botchergate in 1927 for thirty or so years until they ceased trading. Housewives today would welcome the 'absolutely pure new quality Maypole margarine for 6d' at such a reasonable price! Cooper & Company, grocers, were only a couple of doors away on the Victoria viaduct, and Lipton Ltd, dairy supplies, were across the road in English Street, thus giving rise to the nickname the 'Greasy Corner'.

Crowds throng the Green Market on a market day, which was either Wednesday or Saturday, *c.* 1880. As the street name denotes, this was used for the sale of vegetables. On the far left the windows of the Guildhall are visible and in the centre is the chemist's shop of Henry Sawyer, standing on the corner of Fisher Street and St Alban's Row, which goes down to the right. The end of the Town Hall is on the right, with the clock above.

Henry Sawyer MPS, the owner of the chemist's shop, was born on 18 October 1851 and died on 28 August 1926. He started his business at an early age and was a pharmacist in the city throughout his life. His premises moved to other sites, its last position being in a shop on the extreme left of the picture above. It is still run in his name although different owners have had it since his death.

Regarding the great, worldwide empire of Laing plc, Carlisle is proud to remember that it was the humble beginning here from which the local stonemason started. By the turn of the century Laing had become a well-established firm and in 1907 they built their first department store in Carlisle for Robinson Brothers, later to be taken over by Binns and then House of Fraser. Robinson Bros had a grand arcade and Jacobean café as well as being complete house furnishers and outfitters; and they delivered all their goods free of charge.

A bill head for W. Wright & Sons, English Street, Carlisle, March 1915. A fine building in those days, it was even more elegant in 1745 when, as the home of a Mr Highmore, Bonnie Prince Charlie stayed there on his triumphant march south, proclaiming his father King of England at Carlisle Cross. His advance was halted, however, and he was soon fleeing north. The site of this historic house is now the store of Marks & Spencer.

The large staff of Marks & Spencer Ltd line up outside their shop in English Street which in those days was between their present store and the Victoria viaduct. They were advertising 'business as usual' while extensive additions were carried out, but the enlarged store would be open shortly and admission was free. Designated a bazaar, it was very different from the prestigious store we know today.

Thomas Underwood, the mineral water manufacturer, used a horse and cart to deliver his crates of minerals around the town for many years. Here they are loaded up and ready for the off outside the premises in Junction Street, probably in the 1920s.

As well as having their general drapery department under the Guildhall on the Green Market, J. Huthart & Co. had a shop for their gents' mercery at the top of Fisher Street, next door to the corner shop of Sawyer's, the chemists, in the 1920s. The sign on the wall shows they were agents for Pullars of Perth dye works. The entrance to Rosemary Lane is on the extreme left.

When the Government-run Control Board took over the management of all licensed premises in Carlisle in 1916 they closed a third of the 100 public houses in the city at that time. They improved others and also opened eating places. This is the interior of the Gretna Tavern in Lowther Street which was opened by the Earl of Lonsdale on 12 July 1916.

Mr W. Wilson and his staff at his shoeing forge in West Walls, Carlisle, with a coachman at the rear waiting for his horse to be shod. Jackie on the right was Mr Wilson's right-hand man. Behind the closed doors were four furnaces. Mr Wilson, who was born at Lingey Close, Dalston, on 1 February 1857, and died in 1933, had the largest shoeing and stabling premises in Cumberland. He had the contract for all the railway horses, which he both shod and attended in a veterinary capacity, and he was considered one of the finest judges of horseflesh in the north. He was a familiar figure, travelling round Carlisle in his gig drawn by Mountain Maid, who was thirty-four when her master died. In her younger days she never let a motor car pass her down Warwick Road and left trams far behind.

Only two small houses separated Mr Wilson's shoeing forge from the registered office of the wholesale fruit merchants and importers, W.B. Anderson & Sons Limited, at 77 West Walls, Carlisle. Taking advantage of the sunshine some of the staff have come downstairs in their lunch hour to pose for the camera in 1952. From left to right: Elizabeth Bury (author), Ina Finlay, Elizabeth McArdle, Molly Smith, Maree Scott, Sybil Graham and, seated on the ground, Etta Hartley.

Do today's cattle arrive at auction in a more excitable state of mind after being pushed into a cattle waggon and jolted along the road, rather than walking there in a leisurely manner? These prized bulls are warmly wrapped up against the cold as they proudly lead the herd up Warwick Road, probably going to the auction mart of Messrs Hetherington in Earl Street in about 1905.

Two brothers, William and John Pratchitt, started the general engineers and iron founders works, known as Pratchitt Bros, at Denton Works in 1859. Coming into Denton Street from the city it was the first building on the right-hand side. Here some of the men are busily employed at the works in the early part of this century.

Stan Robson was born at Moss Head, five miles from Hethersgill, in 1906. Always interested in transport, he converted a car into a van to take his first load in 1925, expanding into Robson's Border Transport, the names of all vehicles being prefixed by 'Border'. He encountered difficulties in the depression of the early 1930s, and again in the Second World War, but by 1958 he had a fleet in excess of 100 vehicles and carried 1,000 tons a day. In 1980 the company was acquired by United Glass Group and combined to form Robson's Distribution Services. A familiar figure to all his workers, Stan Robson, in the cap he was rarely seen without, gives some last-minute instructions to the driver of 'Border Dandy' as he prepares to leave with his loaded wagon.

A 1918 Model T Ford, registration number XL 453, called 'Border Veteran', which Stan Robson always kept as a reminder of his early days, stands in the place of honour with the fleet lined up behind at the depot at Harraby, Carlisle.

The hard water of the River Caldew made it particularly suitable for bleaching and one of the cotton print works that took advantage of this was Stead McAlpin at their factory at Cummersdale. Block printers from the firm, seen here in about 1894 are, back row, from left to right: Mat Collins, father of Jimmy Collins who died in New Zealand in the 1970s, Bob Pollard, grandfather of Sid and Herbert Pollard, Jacob Brough Stewart and John Stewart. Front row: Kit Watson, an unknown boy, and George Bonner.

Employees at the print works of Stead McAlpin & Co. Ltd, Cummersdale, using the two-trolley system. As the material passes from them it rises up on the right of the picture, giving some idea of the very attractive chintz patterns produced by the firm.

For over a century and a half the name Carr's Biscuits was synonymous with Carlisle. James Dodgson Carr started a bakery in Castle Street, Carlisle, in 1831, moving to larger premises in Caldewgate in 1834 as his business expanded. The firm steadily increased in size with its own railway line coming in from the canal goods yard on the right of this picture, which was taken from the top of the joiner's shop. Just visible against the centre skyline is the spire of Holy Trinity Church, whose commanding island position was only a street's width from Carr's frontage. In 1947 the spire was removed for safety reasons, the church being demolished in 1982 because it was also unsafe.

A young worker at Carr's around the turn of the century. The very familiar pack of Carr's Cream Crackers and the smaller one of Carr's Colonial biscuits signifies the worldwide market that their biscuits had now reached.

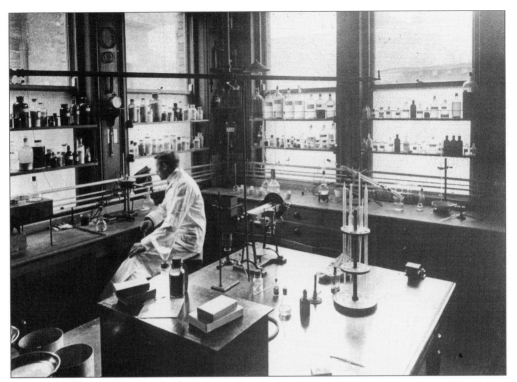

The technical side of the biscuit business was conducted in Carr's well-equipped laboratory, pictured here, probably in the 1920s.

Biscuits in the making at the Carlisle factory of Carr & Co., *c.* 1908. Today's mechanization and the speed with which goods are produced and packed would have been beyond the imaginations of those working long hours and repetitive jobs, nearly ninety years ago.

Mr G. Thompson and the staff of the ledger department of Carr & Co., Carlisle, at the annual staff party, *c.* 1931. This was held at Newbiggin Hall, the home of Colonel Ronald Carr, a delightful old country house just south of the city.

Carr & Co. were always known as caring employers, providing good amenities for their workers. Their canteen was in Morton Street, on the opposite side of Caldewgate, and was quite spacious with a garden area. Here some of the staff are entertaining wounded servicemen during the Second World War.

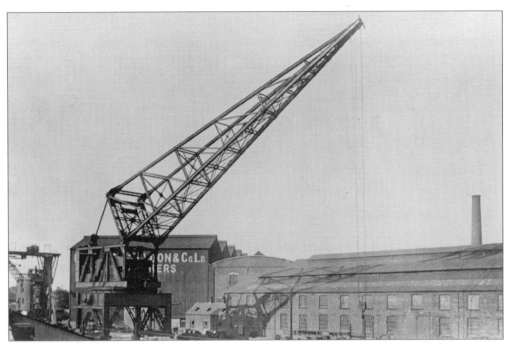

John Cowans and Edward Pattison Sheldon founded the firm of Cowans, Sheldon & Company at Woodbank, near Upperby, in 1846, moving to St Nicholas, between London Road and the railway, in 1859. They were an outstanding firm of crane builders, predominantly rail suppliers for all parts of the world. Sheldon had served his apprenticeship with Robert Stephenson & Company and, on their behalf, drove the first locomotive to enter Carlisle when the railway from Newcastle was opened in about 1836. Sadly, the process of closing the firm down began in 1987, the engineering capacity being transferred to Tyneside. The site is now being completely redeveloped with business units.

The staff of Cowans, Sheldon & Company pictured at the St Nicholas works, probably in the early part of the century. It is noticeable that all the men wear caps except the boss or foreman on the extreme right, who is wearing a bowler hat.

The Electric Lighting Station in James Street, Carlisle, was built by Laings in 1899 and opened by the mayor, George White, to supply electricity for domestic and street lighting. The original inscription and coat of arms of the city are still visible, although covered by a notice advertising the present use of the building which is the Carlisle Enterprise Centre. With the number of electricity users rapidly expanding, a new power station was built at Willow Holme in 1925.

Horses played a very large part in the construction industry at Laings in the early years, all bricks and mortar being moved by horse and cart until the end of the First World War. It was not until 1951 that the last of the horses finished at Laings' premises in Dalston Road, Carlisle. Bob Pickup, the carter, is seen here with one of the horses he worked with to the end. He obviously had a great feeling for them.

The Cumberland and Westmorland Institution for the Blind was established in 1956 with workshops for the blind opening in 1872, a building being erected for this purpose on the south side of Lonsdale Street in 1878–9. This photograph, showing those employed at the workshop, was taken at those premises in about 1890. Through the archway on the left can be seen the shops on the opposite side of the street and on the right-hand side are piled up some of the baskets that they made, along with mattresses and mats.

'The two Alfs.' Mr Alfred Brisco, who had succeeded his father as director of the National Equine Defence League, with one of the pit ponies they cared for, also called Alf, at their premises at Blackwell, Carlisle. Founded in 1909, the League does tremendous work caring for any animal in need and now has spacious accommodation at Wetheral Shields, just south of the city.

The Carlisle postal staff in 1912, the location possibly being one of the town bowling greens. The number of employees may seem large, especially as they were still in the smaller Lowther Street premises, but they did have to deal with all the telegrams and parcels that passed through a sizeable city.

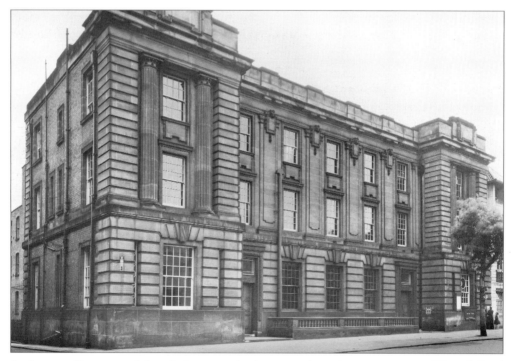

As the post office operated the telephones coming into general use, larger premises on Warwick Road were designed in 1912. The contract was awarded to Laings in 1913 and it was opened in 1915. It has since been refurbished in 1980, again by Laings.

MAKING GLAD WITH MUSIC

A very popular occupation towards the end of the nineteenth century and into the early twentieth century was to sit in Victoria Park, Carlisle, and listen to the the band concerts. There were many local bands and what could be pleasanter on a warm day than to meet friends and listen to good music.

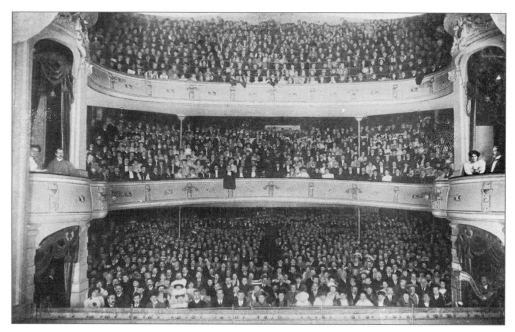

After using various buildings for stage productions a purpose-built theatre was erected in 1874, known as the Victoria Hall but later becoming Her Majesty's Theatre in Lowther Street. Unfortunately a disastrous fire in 1904 meant that the whole of the interior had to be rebuilt. A capacity audience is enjoying a performance of *Maritana* by the Moody Manners Opera Company on 23 February 1907, two years after its reopening.

The band of the Carlisle and District Province of the Royal Antediluvian Order of Buffaloes, seen early this century. It is many years since the Order had a band in Carlisle but they have a flourishing club with a membership of 850 in their spacious premises in Fisher Street.

Many works and organizations had their own bands and this is the GPO Boys' Band. Some of the telegraph delivery boys look very young, many recent school leavers, no doubt. This picture was possibly taken early in the century in Crosby Street, behind the old Lowther Street post office before it moved to Warwick Road in 1916.

The handbell team of the Willow Holme Mission taken in the 1930s by Mr F.W. Tassell in his Lowther Street studio. Standing, left to right: Willie Cowen, Isabel Brown, Jimmy Skinner, Mildred Ashbridge, Tommy Pattinson (the leader). Seated in front are Molly Bell and Elizabeth Brown who, sadly, is the only one still living. All keen members of the team, they used to meet weekly for practice as well as frequently going out to give concerts. Mr Hutchinson, manager of Carr's Biscuits, who led the Mission, had borrowed the handbells, seen here on the table, from Quaker friends. After the team disbanded the bells went to the Salvation Army for a while but were later returned to the Quakers.

The Music Festival was an important event in the social calendar of Carlisle each spring and the day when the rural choirs competed was particularly enjoyable. After months of rehearsing they came from all over North Cumberland in hopeful anticipation. After singing the set pieces and being filled with the joy of success or crestfallen by the adjudicator's remarks, all the choirs united for a concert in the evening. Here the choirs are assembled in the Drill Hall, Strand Road, on 7 March 1923.

Mr William Henry Reid, headmaster of the Bishop Goodwin School on Blackwell Road, which was built in 1892, was well known in the city for his musical ability and leadership. He is pictured with the school choir on 28 May 1912, along with the trophies they won on their recent visit to the International Musical Festival in Paris. They achieved first prize in sight-reading and a second in another class. A band turned out to welcome them home only to discover they had missed the train in London. Nothing dismayed this band, however, and they were back at the station when the choir finally arrived at 2 a.m. They must have woken many citizens up as 'See the Conquering Hero Come' rang through the streets with terrific gusto.

The members of Carlisle City Police Band in 1905. The gentleman in the centre wearing a top hat is George Hill Esq., the chief constable, with Superintendent Eckford on his right. Sergeant W.J. Sinton, bandmaster, is seated on Mr Hill's left and Sergeant Burnett, secretary, is sitting on the left of the picture. The small boy sitting on the floor looks rather apprehensive at being surrounded by the law.

Most of the Carlisle churches had, and still have, very active branches of the Boys' Brigade. Looking very smart the battalion band marches over Caldew Bridge from their headquarters in Abbey Street to Holy Trinity Church, led by Drum Major W. Thursby in the 1950s. A cattle waggon tries to overtake them while the castle keep is visible on the left. The houses on the right were demolished for road widening in 1973–4.

Carlisle Salvation Army Band outside the Market Street entrance to the covered market in 1927. Back row, left to right: T. Bradley, J. Fell, W. James, F. Nixon, J. Stewart, R. West and T. Nicholson. Second row: H. Armstrong, J. Abba, T. Barnes, E.D. Saunders, W. Rayson, W. Casson, J. Taylor, J. McDonald and R. Scott. Third row: R. Nicholson, P. Kerr, W. Wield, E. Nicholson, J. Lorimer, C. Lowes and R. Lowes. Seated: G. Armstrong, S. Little, J. Hill, R. Wield, W. Lowes (bandmaster, standing), W. Fell, J. Nicholson and F. Watt.

The band of Harraby Hill House Home, c. 1905. Hill House was known as the children's workhouse but there must have been much musical talent among ones so young to have such a good band.

Children's bands have always been quite a novelty and this one belonged to Denton Holme Conservative Club. This picture was taken in Morley Street School yard with Mr DeColt seated in the centre, *c.* 1931. The school premises are no longer used as such but the buildings still stand and are used for community purposes.

St Stephen's Silver Band outside Carlisle Grammar School. Back row, from left to right: -?-, -?-, -?-, -?-, W. James, F. Nixon, E. Saunders, W. Rayson, T. Barnes, -?-, -?-, -?-. Centre row: W. Kerr (drum), H. Routledge, R. West, H. Armstrong, E. Nicholson, W. Casson, R. Lowes, J. Lorimer, W. Routledge, R. Scott and W. Fell (drum). Front row: -?-, E. Nicholson, S. Hardisty, W. Lowes, G. Armstrong, J. Nicholson, -?-. The great number of trophies the band won over the years for outstanding playing are displayed in front of Mr W. Lowes, the bandmaster. In 1927, and again in 1929, they came first in the British Band Federation Thousand Guinea Trophy at Crystal Palace. On their first success in London Mr Lowes, a brilliant musician but a most unassuming man, is said to have left the train at Penrith on the return journey rather than face the tremendous ovation that was waiting for them in Carlisle.

John Allen playing the fiddle at Redhill, opposite Old Hall, Rockcliffe. A stoneknapper by trade, he was well known in that area during the 1900s and died in the 1930s. Whatever else he did, he was most particular about having clean and shining boots.

EDUCATIONAL & SPORTING ACTIVITIES

Players come out on to the pitch for a match at Edenside, the home of Carlisle cricket club, in the 1920s.
Cricket has been played here since the game came to the city early in the nineteenth century.

The grassy slope rising from the cricket ground made an ideal arena for spectators and was a very pleasant place to sit on a summer's day with the view over the river and the city beyond. Play is in progress here in about 1910. The row of houses towards the right is Eden Terrace, which was demolished in 1930 to allow for the widening of the bridge over the River Eden. Very attractive gardens were laid out on part of the site.

Valentine, a competitor in the 1911 Circuit of Britain Air Race, arrived in Carlisle on Wednesday 26 July of that year at 4.22 p.m. at The Swifts. After checking in he was driven in a Napier car by his friend Oscar C. Morson to the Crown & Mitre Hotel where he is seen arriving, waving to the cheering crowds. Sadly, a year or so later, he died following an operation for appendicitis, when he was on a visit to the Continent.

Holy Trinity Church, Carlisle, 1st Company of Boy Scouts in 1919. The Reverend R. Davenport, curate of Holy Trinity Church and a master at Carlisle Grammar School, is the scoutmaster seated in the centre. He later became vicar of Scotby and an Honorary Canon of Carlisle Cathedral.

The swimming team from the Bishop Goodwin School, Currock, around the time of the First World War. The master is Mr Joe Scales from Cumdivock, Dalston, and the tall boy on his left is William Gash of Clementina Terrace, Currock, who later became headteacher at Stanwix School.

The members of Carlisle United AFC for the 1906–7 season. Standing, left to right: C.K. Coulthard (chairman), A. Clark, W. Blyth (captain), J. Scott, A. Carter, R. Spottiswood, J. Hind (trainer) and W.C.G. Hetherington (president). Seated: F. Smith, G. Thomson, G. Pickering, H. Lyon, T. Sanderson and A. Gardner.

The members of St Stephen's AFC in 1921, one of many such groups of keen players. Judging from the photo there appear to be as many aspiring players as team members.

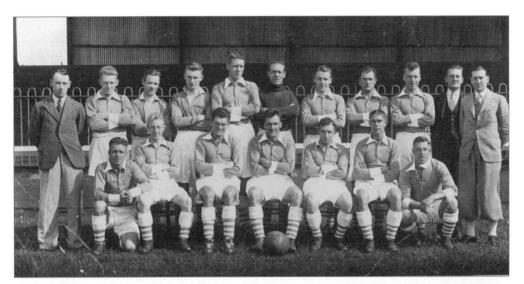

The members of Carlisle United AFC for the 1935–6 season. Standing, left to right: Charlie Parker (trainer), Lloyd, James, Hill, Bound, Harland, Manus, Webster, Henderson, William Clarke (secretary) and Bob Kelly (manager). Seated: Kerr, Williams, Landells, Shankley, Galloway, Cliffe and Johnston.

Many of the local firms had their own football team and the print works at Cummersdale was no exception. Their team had been set up during short time working by apprentice block printers; this meant that when the firm could not get enough orders to have full employment for everyone, the workers were all put on fewer hours per week rather than pay some off. This way they were still available when full employment returned. They are photographed here in 1932. Back row, left to right: Chris Pullen (secretary), Joe Clarke, John Stewart, George Baker, Joe Kirkpatrick, Albert Wilkinson, Bill Stewart and John Pattinson. Seated: John Nicholson, Tom Pullen, John Beaty, Harold Beaty and Bob Blair. Sitting on the grass, with the ball proudly held between his feet, is Fred Rogerson.

The Mayor of Carlisle presenting the Hospital Cup to the captain of the local butchers' team in 1906, while an eager crowd look on. Seated on the far left is James Little, captain of Carlisle Volunteer Firemen and on the board of governors for the hospital.

Attendance at evening classes for commercial and secretarial training has long been an established habit, as shown by the young people here around the turn of the century, but the young ladies seem to be in the majority in this group. The modern technology of today's typewriters and computers are a world of difference away from the machines in use at this time.

Neat and tidy, with well-polished shoes, children of the Fawcett School in West Walls are happy to be photographed during the early part of the century. The Fawcett School was built in 1851 for 322 boys and 257 girls so was quite a large school. As people tended to live further from the city centre, the schools moved and the Fawcett School became redundant and now no longer exists.

Morley Street School in Denton Holme was a junior school for both boys and girls. It was built in 1880, enlarged in 1885 and again in 1894 to accommodate 912 children. Here some of the infants look rather apprehensively at the camera in the late nineteenth century while the little one in the right-hand bottom corner proudly holds up the name of the class.

Miss E. Allonby on the left and Miss J.A. Tinkler on the right, with their two assistant teachers sitting on either side of them, are pictured with their pupils at the private school they ran at their home, Ingledene, 112 Warwick Road, Carlisle (on the corner of Lismore Street) in the latter part of the 1930s. The school provided full education for girls as well as junior boys.

Kilncroft School for boys, c. 1957–8. Miss Elton, the headmistress, is seated in the centre together with members of staff. Guy Pawle, fourth from the right, is the photographer for Tullie House Museum. Some of his work is used to illustrate local books.

The pupils of Carlisle Preparatory School, 14 Victoria Place, in 1932. The headmaster at that time was David Staines BA, and the photographer was F.W. Trassel. He had a studio in Lowther Street.

The Robert Ferguson School in Denton Holme was built to accommodate 360 senior mixed pupils and 360 infants. Some of the pupils are gathered here, probably in the 1930s, in the costumes worn for a play or pageant they were staging.

Bowls has, for many years, been the very popular game that it still is today. One can almost feel the heat of the sun as these players, mostly in shirt sleeves, make momentous decisions regarding the position of the bowls at a club in Carlisle in the 1930s.

The members of Stanwix Bowling Club in 1880 on the green on which they played behind Mrs Swallow's public house, the Bird-in-Hand, in Rickergate. It was 1901 before the green in Stanwix was opened. They are, back row, left to right: -?- (grocer), B. Stephenson (jeweller), Herbert Gill (Brampton), Mr Baxter (joiner), Mr Brown (gentleman), -?- (brewer's traveller), Mr Hewitson (Stanwix stock and sharebroker with Mr Kennedy, Devonshire Street), Mr Bulman (city surveyor's assistant, Stanwix), Mr Bob Heslop (Stanwix), Mr Caddle (confectioner), -?- (Stanwix). Centre row: Mr Little, Mr Wilson (jeweller), Mr Elwin (schoolmaster), Mr Howard (grocer, Market Place, Glover's Row), -?- (Flemings Buses), Mr Armstrong (joiner), -?- (Stanwix). Front row: -?- (Edentown), -?- (hatter), -?-, Mr N. Thompson (Abbey Street), Mr Jim Riley, -?-, -?- (Hetherington's Marts), -?-.

The picture of this large group of people was presented to Stanwix Bowling Club by their first committee; the club was opened on 16 May 1901 by His Worship, the Mayor of Carlisle, John Hurst, Esq. The president of the club was Jos Brown, the Vice-President, C. Stuart, Treasurer, G. Wills, Secretary, F. Cox, and on the committee were A. Blakeley, Thos. Graham, W.H. Reeves, J. Pattinson, A. Grieve, R. Ward, John Reeves, J.J. Townson and J. Laidlow.

Play is being enjoyed on three rinks at Stanwix Bowling Club in the early years of the century. The bushes at the back of the green, bordering on the main road running north from the city, have grown somewhat. The houses in the background are Eden Mount on the west side of Scotland Road.

J. McCALL   G.WILLS. W.H.REEVES.   R.HOLMES.

Time for discussion on the state of play or perhaps a welcome break: J. McCall, G. Wills, W.H. Reeves and R. Holmes do not seem too concerned about the placing of the woods and the jack. Another member views the situation from the doorway of the bower.

SERVICE TO THE CITY

A steam lorry stands in English Street at the entrance to St Cuthbert's Lane unloading beer barrels, possibly for the Fish & Dolphin public house just up the lane. L. Sanderson, whom the owners of the lorry are supporting, stood as a Conservative candidate in the by-election of 1905 and was beaten by F.W. Chance, the Liberal candidate. The total electorate at that time was 7,344, Chance getting 3,616 votes and Sanderson 2,586.

The number of policemen placed on duty outside Charlotte Street Congregational Church for the by-election on 14 July 1905 makes it look as though they are expecting disorder. Perhaps there were more on the force then or they may have just congregated for the photograph.

F.W. Chance (later Sir Frederick), beat L. Sanderson in the by-election caused by the elevation to the peerage of the sitting member – the Right Honourable W.C. Gully QC, being created Viscount Selby. There is no doubt whom this wagon is supporting as it passes the entrance to Tait Street on its way south down Botchergate. In the election of 1906 F.W. Chance was returned unopposed and after that he did not stand for Parliament again.

As the placards proclaim 'Hurrah for Howard' and 'Your Old Member', the Hon. G.W.A. Howard is conveyed into Carlisle after winning the North Cumberland seat for the Liberals at the election on 21 January 1910. He beat C.W.H. Lowther (Conservative) by 4,504 votes to 4,470. The figures at the previous election in 1906 had been fairly similar; 4,467 for Howard and 4,230 for Lowther. In spite of it being January there was no shortage of supporters standing on the street to greet him.

Major-General E.L. Spears (later Sir Edward) was elected Member of Parliament for Carlisle on 28 October 1931, with a majority of 4,634, having been unsuccessful at the last election. He remained an MP until 1945 when he was beaten by Edgar Grierson. Here Mrs Sutcliffe, wife of Councillor Sutcliffe, is opening a garden fête in their home at Houghton Hall, supported by the Reverend Tom Brown, vicar of Houghton, on her right and General Spears on her left, in the mid-1930s.

A charming photograph as Ron Lewis's wife, Edna, ensures his rosette is correctly positioned. Ron Lewis worked for British Rail in the wagon maintenance shops near Crewe and, after a request from Carlisle Labour Party for a nominee as a Parliamentary candidate from the railway, he was nominated by the Railway Union to stand in 1961. He was elected in 1962 and remained as Member of Parliament for Carlisle until his retirement in 1985. A very popular MP, his firm Christian convictions shone through all his deeds and words, not least as an active Methodist lay-preacher.

With great solemnity the sword and macebearers lead the mayor, aldermen and councillors from the cathedral in Carlisle after attending a civic service in about 1905. In those days no women were members of the Council. The civic procession still regularly makes its way to the cathedral for special occasions, the mayor having his own stall there and wearing the same chain of office, with the sword and mace carried before him, but now he is accompanied by the mayoress and the Council is probably composed of as many women as men.

The Bishop of Carlisle, the Right Reverend J.W. Diggle (bishop from 1905 to 1920), walks away from an interesting discussion outside the courts in Carlisle. He leaves behind Sir James Watt of Knowefield, Stanwix, Mr Mounsey Heysham (with the buttonhole) of Castledown, Rockcliffe, and two unknown others.

Knowefield, Stanwix, was situated off the right-hand side of Scotland Road, going north at the edge of the city. The home of Sir James Watt JP, it was in its extensive grounds that the nursery was run for the old established seed merchants, Little & Ballantyne, of which he was the head. The house has been demolished since the Second World War and the whole area is now developed for housing.

A long procession of men walk behind the two horse-drawn hearses carrying the coffins of the driver and fireman from one of the trains involved in the Gretna train disaster in 1915. Coming from St Ann's it was a long walk to Stanwix Cemetery, on the road north not far from Kingstown, where they were buried.

In the days of horse-drawn vehicles the water trough at the roadside was as important as the petrol station is today for the motorist. With due ceremony this trough was placed on Kingstown Road, north of the city. The inscription read, 'In Grateful Remembrance of Priscilla Hannah Johnston of the Beeches, Rickerby, and of her work for Animals, Here and in Distant Lands. Erected by Friends and Neighbours, 1913. I am poor and needy but the Lord careth for me.' With modern developments, road widening and the end of horse traffic the trough became obsolete and was moved by workmen. It was found in a Council yard a few years ago, restored and relettered and brought to Rickerby where it stands near to the home of the one in whose memory it was placed and where the residents take great pride in keeping it full of flowering plants.

WAYS OF TRAVEL

*When the main north-south railway line was built in 1847 the very fine Citadel station was built to cater
for passengers. No fewer than seven different railway companies ran into Carlisle but gradually the new
station became the terminal for them all. Cabs line up in Court Square waiting for the arrival of passengers
around the turn of the century, the small building in the centre giving the cabbies rest and warmth between
fares, while foot passengers make for the trains. The County & Station Hotel is the large building on the left,
now known as the Cumbria Hotel.*

John Menzies' bookstall was always a popular place on the platform at Carlisle station and passengers were able to jump out to buy a paper while the train made a more leisurely stop than is the case today. When the main line trains stopped the stationmaster was always there in a top hat, every inch the gracious dignitary. Looking north here there is a train standing in the double bay from which they left for Silloth and Langholm.

Two engines are steamed up ready to haul the express, which has just come from Scotland, on its way over Shap. Whether the dog in the centre has alighted or is merely there to meet a visitor, it seems unconcerned by the noise and plumes of smoke.

A Midland engine steams up as it prepares to leave Carlisle station. This locomotive was the one used in the Carlisle to Leeds trials in 1923. There is a picture of it in the 1919 to 1939 books of British locomotives by O.S. Nock.

The different railway companies running into Carlisle started to form their own unions of railway servants, as they used to be called, the first branch, Carlisle No. 1, being formed in 1873. No. 2 followed in 1896, No. 3 in 1911, both Nos 4 and 6 in 1913 (No. 5 being the branch for the United Bus Services, which were originally owned by the railways), No. 7 in 1920 and No. 8 in 1923. In 1913 Carlisle had 1,670 members of the union out of a national total of 170,000. In 1926 all the Carlisle branches came together to form one branch of the National Union of Railwaymen, here proudly displaying their very fine new banner depicting the cathedral and the castle under which are clasped hands and the words 'Unity is Strength'. The first secretary for the NUR was Joe Henderson, seated first on the left, a goods guard from No. 3 branch, where he was also secretary. Mr Henderson was the first Labour mayor of Carlisle in 1927 and was elected Member of Parliament for Ardwick in June 1931, later becoming a Government Whip. He was President of the NUR from 1934 to 1936 and was elevated to the House of Lords in 1950. Tragically, he died on 26 February 1950, aged sixty-five, having just taken his seat in the Lords. Tommy Balfour, an engine driver from the canal branch, succeeded Joe Henderson as secretary of the NUR in 1930.

The North British Railway locomotive, no. 374, in Carlisle station on 4 September 1906, having just come under the Viaduct Bridge. In the top right-hand corner the Viaduct Hotel is visible and next to it is the Central Hotel.

Wetheral station, on the Carlisle to Newcastle line, four miles east of Carlisle, presents a very different scene from what it does today. The number of staff, complete with porter and baggage trolley to handle all heavier cases and boxes, is in complete contrast to the now unmanned halts with payment on the train. At least this line does still function.

A North British Railway train leaving Carlisle Citadel station en route for Edinburgh, *c.* 1910. In the bay on the left-hand side, passengers are boarding a train for a more local destination.

A tram makes its way along English Street, passing the statue of the Earl of Lonsdale erected in 1845 between the two Court Houses. The wall on the left is the corner of the gaol and next to it is the City Arms public house, commonly known as the 'Gaol Tap'. The whole block was demolished in 1928 for street widening and new shops.

A horse-drawn omnibus at the top of Newtown Road with Coledale Hall Farm in the background, *c.* 1898. The route was from Boundary Road via the Town Hall and infirmary. It must have been a nice day for the passengers seem to prefer to be outside, probably for a better view.

Electric trams were introduced into Carlisle in 1900, running on the same routes as the horse-drawn omnibuses. Here tram no. 7 is approaching the terminus at the top of Newtown. Gibbon's Terrace is on the left and Coledale Farm is just visible behind the tram. This would be about ten years later than the picture above.

At about the same time, a tram makes its way west from the city centre through Caldewgate, passing the Liberal Institute in the centre of the picture. This tram is advertising waterproofs from the Carlisle Rubber Co., 30 Lowther Street.

D. Asti of Bridge Street, Caldewgate, had a car in the early days of motoring, probably in about 1920, to ply his ice cream trade. On the side of the car is written, 'When you want a cooler, try D. Asti Famous Ices'.

A charabanc trip was the highlight of the season in the 1920s. This one is well filled and ready for the off with a great display of fashionable headgear by the ladies. A windy day might have caused concern although the charabanc would hardly appear to be moving very speedily. Only the spare tyre was carried so, if unfortunate enough to have a puncture which was not infrequent in those days, the tyre had to be changed and not just the wheel.

Passengers wait to board the tram on its return journey back to Carlisle at the bottom of Etterby Street looking up towards Stanwix. The hedge on the left has now been cleared to make a road into the housing development.

The *Daily Mail* Circuit of Britain Air Race of 1911 caused great excitement, nowhere more so than in Carlisle which had been selected as a control stop. The race started from Brooklands on 22 July, the first competitor arriving in Carlisle on 25 July amid great acclaim and excitement. Others followed in the next day or so but it was not until 1 August that Colonel Cody arrived on The Swifts, the official landing ground. He had actually come the previous day by train from Lanark, where his plane was undergoing repair, to ask the timekeeper to keep the books open one more day. Mr Fattorini agreed to this and here he is signing Colonel Cody into Carlisle.

Valentine tries his engine before leaving Carlisle on 28 July 1911 in the Circuit of Britain Air Race. He had arrived in Carlisle on the 26 July but high winds had prevented him leaving on the 27th.

An event which aroused much interest was an air display at Kingstown, on the northern outskirts of Carlisle, on 10 August 1933. As in the days of early motoring, planes, like cars, were started by hand. Here the propellors are being swung for the Hon. Mrs Victor Bruce, seated in the aircraft, to take off on a stunt flight. The site became a RAF flying training school during the war and is now a large industrial estate.

Miss Dorothy N. Spicer, mechanic, and Miss Pauline Gower, pilot, join the public at the refreshment van at the air display, Kingstown. One small boy, complete with cap, regards them with awe and wonder while another boy walks away unconcerned.

In the 1920s numerous omnibus operators began to take over from the trams in providing transport around the city. Here the driver and conductor of a no. 54 wait by their vehicle in the market-place, ready to leave for their route up Wigton Road to the new estate at Raffles.

The market square in the 1920s showing a number of omnibuses, each of which had their own pick-up point for passengers. The Market Cross is on the left, the Town Hall on the right and the Crown & Mitre Hotel in the centre at the back.

One of the first motorized charabancs in the district, registration number AO 4652, was owned by Mr Millican of Hethersgill in the early 1920s. With the splendid name of 'Border Queen', it had solid tyres and a sheet of canvas for a roof but there were seats for all who wanted to ride. It doubled up as the post bus and Mr Millican was in Carlisle by 5.45 a.m. every morning to collect the post for delivery to Houghton, Scaleby, Smithfield and Roadhead, collecting for a return run every evening. Mr Millican's daughter married Stan Robson who developed Robson's Border Transport and was so impressed with the name 'Border Queen' that all the names of his vehicles were prefixed by 'Border'.

Millican's bus depot in East Tower Street, Carlisle, in premises that had previously belonged to James Nixon. A young lady waiting the arrival of the charabanc looks out of the double-fronted premises. They had a waiting room on one side and a room reserved for ladies on the other.

The horse-drawn conveyance which belonged to the Crown & Mitre Hotel was a familiar sight on the streets, taking guests from railway station to hotel and back. The horseman is on the box ready to set off from the spacious hotel yard, situated at the rear of the hotel. The east end of St Cuthbert's Church is the building at the left of the picture. A motor vehicle succeeded the horse but today the yard is used for the guests' own cars.

Joe Bell was a motor proprietor who ran his business at 79 West Walls, Carlisle. Available night and day, he is seen here, probably in the 1930s waiting to collect a passenger with his spotlessly clean car.

SECTION NINE

MEMORABLE HAPPENINGS

There was always great excitement when the circus came to town and everyone stopped to watch the parade through the streets. The camels, not deigning to look left or right, tread haughtily along Castle Street, their riders attired in festive garb, escorted by members of the band – one can be seen on the right on a white horse. This picture dates from the early 1900s.

Caldewgate was an area that was very liable to flood, one of the worst being in January 1925. Looking west Holy Trinity Church stands in the centre complete with spire, before it had to be removed for safety, and the Joiner Arms public house is on the right. Buses, cars and a horse and cart cautiously make their way through the water while spectators gather at the bottom of Wigton Road to watch the scene.

September 1918 was another time of severe flooding in Carlisle and this picture was taken on the 16th, showing the vast area under water when the River Eden burst its banks.

Joyce Irwin and Kathleen Nickson, daughter of the Reverend Ernest Nickson, Vicar of St John the Evangelist Church, London Road, look after a young friend at the garden party in the vicarage garden in the summer of 1937.

The workers at Carr & Co.'s biscuit works enjoy their staff party at the beautiful home and grounds of Colonel Ronald Carr, chairman of the company, c. 1950. He lived at Newbiggin Hall, a few miles south of the city.

The 'Three Graces' enjoy the sunshine at the annual garden party of St John the Evangelist in the vicarage garden on London Road in 1937. From left to right they are, Miss Allonby, Miss Annie Dodd and Miss Tinkler. Miss Allonby and Miss Tinkler ran a private school on Warwick Road. Miss Dodd was a typical Victorian lady with skirts always reaching to the ground. Her house on London Road, not far from the church, of which she was a staunch supporter, was a relic of Victorianism and genteel respectability. Should she be able to return today and see the public house, into which it has been turned, it would not be difficult to imagine the absolute horror with which she would be overcome.

Miss Dorothy Ashburner, younger daughter of
the late Mr Banks Ashburner (grocer) and Mrs
Ashburner of Strand Road, Carlisle, after her
marriage to Squadron Leader Frank Binns at the
Central Hall Methodist Church in Fisher Street
on 20 February 1947. They met during the war
when the bride was driving for the Air Ministry
at 14 MU and the bridegroom was posted there.
The matron of honour on the left is the bride's
sister, Mrs Margaret Wallace, and the best man,
Mr John Moss, is on the right.

John Y. Obertellie takes advantage of the sunshine to sell his ice cream beside the Market Cross while
traders ply their wares from the steps of the cross, c. 1880. The Town Hall windows can be seen either
side of the cross while on the left, behind the ice cream cart, Glover's Row is visible. This was demolished
in 1897, making a much more spacious market square and entrance to Castle Street.

A happy gathering of staff from the many branches between Glasgow and Liverpool of W.B. Anderson & Sons Ltd as they join with most of those from the head office in Carlisle for the annual staff dance in the Crown & Mitre ballroom, Carlisle, on Friday 13 March 1953. On the extreme left is Mr Arthur Sutton (company secretary) and his wife, with Miss Waller (the assistant secretary) behind and further back Mr Jim Hanna (transport manager). Fifth from the left is Mr John Anderson (managing director) and his wife is just behind him.

Pieri Bros of Northumberland Street with their horse and smartly decorated cart, preparing to go out and sell the genuine ice cream they advertised. A familiar sight in pre-Second World War days, the arrival of the cart was of great excitement to children and was often the only way to enjoy ices.

The local drivers of Ribble Motor Services, who operated most of the public service vehicles in and around Carlisle, meet for their annual dinner and presentation of safe driving awards in 1979. Back row, from left to right: Brian Tweedale, Norman Thompson, Peter Brown. Harry Graham, Lawrie Norman, Freddie Clarke, Bob Byres, Steve Roberts, Jimmy Smith, Roland Bell, Raymond Thompson, -?-, Vince Barbour, Ronnie Skelton, Harry Mossop, Freddie Thompson, Colin Woodburn. Second row: John Hetherington, Steve Roberts, a police chief, Isabel Bowman, Mary Morley, the Ribble manager, -?-, Stan Lynch. Front row, Derek Kenny, Don Gordon, Des Ferguson, -?-, Keith McMurdo.

May Day was always celebrated with due pomp at St Stephen's Church of England School, which was behind the church of the same name in James Street. Here the 1916 queen is assembled with her attendants in the yard of the Infant's School. Cissie Field was the one chosen for the honour that year. Daffodils and other spring flowers abounded, the male attendants carrying bunches of them at the end of long poles. Sadly the church and school became redundant and the site is now a petrol station and site for other small businesses.

Trades processions with decorated vehicles were a popular feature, particularly between the two world wars. Here two of them are lined up ready for the off with the castle wall as a backdrop. On the left is the vehicle of Underwood's Mineral Waters, Junction Street, giving prominence to the Union Jack, while on the right is the old Renault car with solid wheels of C.H. Hardisty of Milbourne Crescent who advertised motor and cycle tyres, and tubes sold and repaired.

The castle keep makes a splendid setting for the float of W.B. Anderson of West Walls, whose trade mark 'Double U B' was taken from the initials of the founder of the firm. Their vehicle was turned into a most realistic boat, piled high with banana flats and boxes of fruit of which they were importers and wholesalers. Thomas Nelson is the young midshipman, Jim Hanna (who was transport manager) is the captain and Sid Steele the driver in this 1930s picture – the ship proudly proclaiming 'Service our Speciality'.

REACHING OUT ON
RURAL ROADS

A postman setting off with his bicycle on the daily round from The Square, Dalston, around the turn of the century. The majority of mail, particularly in rural areas, was delivered in this way and continued to be so until well after the end of the Second World War. The co-operative store is the first building on the right and the twelfth-century parish church of St Michael is in the centre of the background.

This fine building in The Square, Dalston, was built in 1888 for Dalston Co-operative Industrial Society. Still owned today by the Cumbrian Co-operative Society Ltd, the rear of the premises was sold some years ago, once being used as the post office and now a newsagent's. The condition of the sale was that no provisions, groceries or drapery could be sold there – in other words anything that was sold in the Co-op. In the left-hand window clothing appears to be hanging on the rail, thus displaying the varied stock in the shop.

The Ivel tractor, registration number AO 385, made by the Ivel Agricultural Motor Co., Biggleswade, and supplied by John Hall of Wigton. It was the first tractor owned by Robert Tinniswood of Rosebank, Dalston, and this ploughing demonstration was given on 21 February 1906, on the land of Mr Charles Jackson, Manor House Farm. It ran at 3 m.p.h. and ploughed an acre in 70 minutes.

Towards the end of the last century the piped water pumped from the River Eden, which had been available in Carlisle since 1848, was becoming insufficient for the expanding city. In 1902 work began on a large reservoir at Castle Carrock, eleven miles to the east of Carlisle, drawing water from the River Gelt. Completed in 1909 the turning on of the water was a very special occasion with a large gathering of city and county officials in August of that year.

After the water had been turned on the party came to Wetheral, four miles east of the city, where a demonstration was given by the Carlisle Volunteer Firemen. This was an exciting occasion in the village; the flags were out and the locals joined the dignitaries to watch. To the children who flocked there it must have been an amazing sight on the village green.

The fine elliptical arch and flanking turrets of the gatehouse, the only building remaining of the Benedictine Priory founded at Wetheral in about 1100 as a cell to York and dedicated to the Holy Trinity and Saints Mary and Constantine. At the Dissolution there were eight monks and revenues were estimated at £117 per annum.

On the eastern side of the River Eden, almost immediately opposite Wetheral, is the pleasant village of Great Corby. The only access between the two villages is the fine bridge, built in 1834, carrying the Carlisle to Newcastle railway with a walkway for foot passengers at one side. All other transport has to go a couple of miles downstream to cross the river at Warwick Bridge.

A young couple in their pony and trap approach along the road from Linstock to Carlisle and pass the north lodge of Rickerby House. This was the home of George Head Head, a banker in Carlisle, who had the lodge built, his arms being visible on the pediment. The entrance to the house is just off the picture on the right-hand side.

Scalesceugh, a large house on the main Carlisle to Penrith road about five miles south of the city, was the home of the Harrison family. Sir James Watt of Knowefield is here seated on the left with others gathered for some special occasion at the house, but none are members of the family.

A roadman is busy trimming the edges of the green along the road through Scotby village at the beginning of the century. The tower of the church can be seen behind the houses on the right. Only three miles from Carlisle Scotby still retains a village atmosphere even with almost continuous building, divided only by the M6. Both the Midland and Newcastle railways pass through the village and both had stations there but now the trains no longer stop.

The interior of All Saints' Church, Scotby, built in 1854 at the sole expense of George Head Head of Rickerby House. In red sandstone in the Pointed style it had an embattled tower containing one bell. The good two-manual organ is seen here, behind the reading desk and the choir stalls.

Is the dog hoping for a drink as the man draws water from the pump in the centre of Tarraby village in the 1890s? This is a reminder of the stringencies before piped water was freely available for all. This attractive halmet lies to the north-east of Carlisle, between Stanwix and Houghton.

As the solitary horse and cart amble north up the main road between Stanwix and Kingstown it is difficult to reconcile this scene with today's ceaseless stream of traffic. Now telephone wires are all underground, the road is much wider and the house on the right has disappeared, the premises of Morrison's superstore bordering the road at that point. The terrace on the left and the small cottage end on to the road on the right still remain standing.

Taking a photograph in 1901 was something to bring these two ladies out to watch. This was the Kingstown post office run by Richard Livingstone on the main road north. The Coach & Horses public house, opposite the entrance to the trading estate, now occupies this site.

Mrs Hoodless ran the post office at Kingstown in this more modern block of houses from 1931 to 1940. It was only a few yards further north from the first picture and still on the main road. The post office today is only a couple of doors away.

A horse and cart load up to take deliveries out from the co-operative stores and post office in the centre of Houghton village early this century. Children could play quite safely on the roads in those days. The thatch on the pretty cottage to the right used to be quite a common form of roofing.

Thomas Bushby, the well-known Carlisle artist, captured the spirit of life on the farm at hay time with this painting of Upperby in 1903. The modern silage tower lacks the charm of the neatly made haystacks on every farm but the work involved meant 'all hands on deck'. The fast expanding city has spread out into this and other rural areas.

Mary Cartner, postmistress at Thursby, and the postman – not forgetting the cat, *c.* 1896. Thursby, six miles west of Carlisle, is on the main route to West Cumbria, although a bypass now relieves the village of much traffic. When this photograph was taken the post office was in Church Row.

Some of the low-lying ground around the Solway Plain is mainly moss, providing good supplies of peat. The cutting, stacking and drying of the sods until they reach the right stage for burning takes a lot of effort, involving whole families. Thomas Bushby, the artist, portrayed something of the task in this picture painted at Todhills, north of Carlisle, in 1903.

STRENGTH IN ADVERSITY

*Troops march out from the shelter of the mighty walls of Carlisle Castle as they go off to camp, c. 1900.
Wives and children stand on the grass to watch them go, perhaps wishing they too could get away from what
must have been a rather dreary life in married quarters in those days.*

The soldiers are in a relaxed mood as the bugle blows at the gatehouse of Carlisle Castle between 1900 and 1905. In its present form the castle has stood for over 800 years and seen many stormy periods throughout the border conflicts. King Edward I enjoyed his visits, but Mary Queen of Scots had no choice in the matter!

The relief which greeted the end of the First World War was tremendous although mingled with sorrow for the many who did not return. The peace celebrations in 1919 attracted large crowds who stood in English Street behind the line of troops and watched from every available balcony and window of the Ceylon Tea Warehouse and shops of John Strong and Redmaynes. In 1931 this building was demolished and replaced by Marks & Spencer. Ferguson's Lane is the opening on the left next to the City Picture House, a corner of which is just visible.

The Home Guard has always given valuable service for the defence of the country and here, in December 1916, are the members of the Morton Platoon.

In the Second World War most parishes in the country and districts in the town, as well as all the larger works, formed their own company of the Home Guard consisting of men who, for various reasons, were exempt from military service. Carr & Co. was a firm who formed such a company, the members of which are seen here.

A rest room for soldiers and sailors was opened in Court Square, Carlisle, in the First World War under the control of the Carlisle Citizens' League whose president was the mayor. It served a useful purpose and provided a welcome haven for servicemen, especially as it was so close to the station. The building, as part of the premises of the County & Station Hotel, was for many years the Rendevous Café, while the building on the left was the end of the Midland Bank Chambers.

A wounded soldier is given a warm reception as he returns to his home village on 30 September 1915. His bravery must have come before him, judging by the cheering crowds and the important-looking dignitaries.

The tragedy of the Gretna rail disaster in 1915 brought many of the injured troops to Carlisle, filling the hospitals to overflowing. Fusehill hospital was one and here the patients well enough to leave their beds gather outside with the nurses. Matron appears to be standing in the centre of the doorway. This hospital is now the City Maternity Hospital.

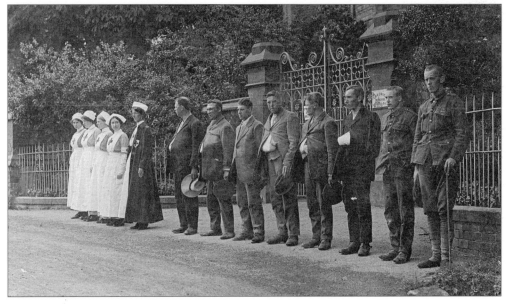

Some of the casualties of the Gretna rail disaster who were well enough to walk line up with their nurses in Carlisle. Mrs Donald, the commandant, is fifth from the left and the others include Miss Boyes, Miss Ferguson and Miss Robinson. Some larger houses were turned into hospitals during the First World War.

Before the Second World War there was no ambulance service as we know it but with the advent of war, local ambulance and rescue personnel were established at different points in the city, to be ready for any contingency and to convey the sick to hospital. One such first aid post was at Trinity School on Port Road, just below Holy Trinity Church, and here all the staff, nurses, drivers and rescue personnel are gathered outside, some wearing tin helmets which were regulation issue.

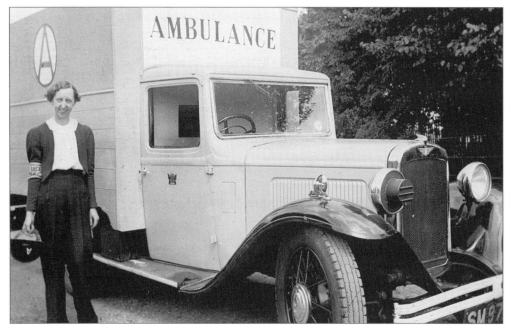

Miss Mary Holmes of Stanwix (fourth from the right on the second row in the above picture) with the ambulance she drove after joining the service on 23 July 1942. At the beginning of the war she had completed a course of anti-gas training and had sufficient knowledge for casualty services. A regulation mask is fitted to one of the ambulance headlamps, the light through the slits of which was all that was permitted in the blackout.

Carlisle Cathedral is the custodian for the colours from many battles and the spiritual base of the Border Regiment. The colour party are lined up outside the south door in 1914 for the laying up of the colours, the choir lined up and the verger ready to escort them.

A dignitary of the church has a word with the troops standing to attention outside the south door of Carlisle Cathedral on the occasion of the laying up of the colours of the Second Battalion of the Border Regiment in the cathedral in August 1914. On the left can be seen the parish church of St Mary which was still functioning then. Now it is a grassy space with an attractive raised round flower bed at the front, designed to mark a special event each year.

As the Second World War progressed, women began to be accepted for work which had previously been the province of men. The lady drivers at no. 14 Maintenance Unit, Royal Air Force were no exception and played an active part in the war effort. Gathered here outside the Unit's main entrance in 1943 are, back row, from left to right: Peggy Bainbridge, Betty Foster, Sally Beckton, Betty Day, Dorothy Bettem, Dorothy Ashburner, Nan Carlton, Elizabeth Bury (author), and Sylvia Day. In front are Mina Fair, Helen Bainbridge, Mr W. Goodey (principal foreman for road transport at the Unit), Betty Cartmel and Audrey Dent.

With the stringencies of war time and lack of entertainment the male drivers at the Unit, numbering about 200, asked the female drivers if they would organize a party at Christmas for their children in 1944. The children appeared to enjoy themselves in the Miles MacInnes Hall at Stanwix and were happy to pose for the photographer. The heavily curtained windows are a reminder that there was a blackout strictly in force.

When peace came in 1945 there was general rejoicing and parties were often held in the street or, as in this one, in a hall or canteen. Everyone gathered together, from the eldest to the youngest, and managed to make a good spread despite all the rationing. The lights went up again in people's hearts as well as in the streets.

The Chadwick Memorial Industrial School, providing education and technical training in different trades for 200 Catholic boys, was in the premises opened as the Convent of the Sacred Heart of Jesus on St Ann's Hill, Stanwix, in September 1882, the school being managed by a community of the Presentation Brothers of Cork. The fine chapel of the Convent was, like a number of buildings, used as an auxiliary hospital during the First World War. The entire building has for some years been the Austin Friars Independent Boarding and Day School and this is the much honoured school chapel.

ACKNOWLEDGEMENTS

The author would like to express her most grateful thanks to everyone who has helped in any way, however small. Collecting photographs from so many sources, it is sometimes extremely difficult to establish copyright and I have tried to contact everyone where names are given but sometimes it has not been possible. So, if anyone sees their photograph and feels offended, I hope they will forgive me and appreciate the pleasure their photo is giving to all who see it.

Particular thanks must go to Bill Boak; Miss Elizabeth Brown; Michael Butcher; Carlisle Public Library; Mrs M. Carverhill; Peter Connon; Cumbrian Newspapers Limited, Carlisle; Councillor Alan Dickinson; Derek Hampson; Dr P. Honeyman; Mr Irving Millican; Colin Johnston; Alan Thorpe and John Laing, plc; Maurice Lightfoot; Eric Martlew MP and Carlisle Labour Party; Mr R. Maxwell; Lawrie Norman; Denis Periam; Anne Simons; Stanwix Bowling Club; Stead McAlpin & Co. Ltd; the late Mr J. Stewart; Mr Strong; Mr Jim Templeton for the use of photographs from the Templeton Collection; Tullie House Museum and Art Gallery; Gerald Watson, Stephen White and Wright, Brown & Strong, solicitors.

My indebtedness especially to Ashley Kendall for allowing me free use of his magnificent collection of postcards, and to Trevor Grahamslaw for his superb photography, making even the oldest photo look good. For their encouragement I am deeply grateful.

Crowds line the street on a warm day. Behind is Robinson's shop with the summer sale in full swing.